TU

SONIDOS
Sort It by SOUND

By Nicholas O'Hara
Traducido por Eida de la Vega

Gareth Stevens
PUBLISHING

conceptos
básicos

Agrupar significa juntar cosas que son parecidas. Puedes agrupar por sonidos.

Sorting means putting things that are alike together. You can sort by sound.

Algunos animales
son ruidosos.

Some animals are loud.

Algunos animales son más callados. Vamos a agrupar por sonidos.

Some animals are quiet. Let's sort by sound.

Los bebés pueden ser
ruidosos o callados.

Babies can be loud
or quiet.

Los bebés que lloran
son ruidosos.

Crying babies are loud.

Los cachorros pueden ser
ruidosos o callados.

Puppies can be loud
or quiet.

Los cachorros dormidos
son silenciosos.

Sleeping puppies
are quiet.

El tiempo puede ser
ruidoso o silencioso.

Weather can be loud
or quiet.

La nieve es silenciosa.

Snow is quiet.

Los autos y los camiones
pueden ser ruidosos
o silenciosos.

Cars and trucks
can be loud or quiet.

12

Un camión de bomberos
es ruidoso.

A fire truck can be loud.

El agua puede ser
ruidosa o silenciosa.

Water can be loud
or quiet.

14

Las olas grandes
son ruidosas.

Big waves are loud.

15

Las aves pueden ser
ruidosas o silenciosas.

Birds can be loud
or quiet.

Los gallos son ruidosos.

Roosters can be loud.

La gente puede ser
ruidosa o callada.

People can be loud
or quiet.

18

Los susurros casi
no se oyen.

Whispers are quiet.

19

La música puede ser
ruidosa o apenas oírse.

Music can be loud
or quiet.

Los tambores
son ruidosos.

Drums can be loud.

21

Mira este parque.
¿Qué cosas piensas que
son ruidosas? ¿Cuáles
son silenciosas?

Look at this park. Which
things do you think are
loud? Which are quiet?

Please visit our website, www.garethstevens.com. For a free color catalog of all our high-quality books, call toll free 1-800-542-2595 or fax 1-877-542-2596.

Library of Congress Cataloging-in-Publication Data

O'Hara, Nicholas.
Sort It by sound = Sonidos / by Nicholas O'Hara.
p. cm. — (Sort it out! = Vamos a agrupar por...)
Parallel title: Vamos a agrupar por...
In English and Spanish.
Includes index.
ISBN 978-1-4824-3221-3 (library binding)
1. Sound — Juvenile literature. I. O'Hara, Nicholas. II. Title.
QC225.5 .O43 2016
534'.078—d23

First Edition

Published in 2016 by
Gareth Stevens Publishing
111 East 14th Street, Suite 349
New York, NY 10003

Copyright © 2016 Gareth Stevens Publishing

Designer: Sarah Liddell
Editor: Therese Shea
Spanish Translation: Eida de la Vega

Photo credits: Cover, p. 1 (polka dots) Victoria Kalinina/Shutterstock.com; cover, p. 1 (instruments) koi88/Shutterstock.com; p. 3 Sergey Novikov/Shutterstock.com; pp. 4, 8 (right) Eric Isselee/Shutterstock.com; p. 5 Tsekhmister/Shutterstock.com; p. 6 (left) Flashon Studio/Shutterstock.com; p. 6 (right) Dmytro Vietrov/Shutterstock.com; p. 7 Boumen Japet/Shutterstock.com; p. 8 (left) WilleeCole Photography/Shutterstock.com; p. 9 oksana2010/Shutterstock.com; p. 10 Nomad_Soul/Shutterstock.com; p. 11 LilKar/Shutterstock.com; p. 12 (left) Maksim Toome/Shutterstock.com; pp. 12 (right), 13 Rob Wilson/Shutterstock.com; p. 14 Ray Esteves/Shutterstock.com; p. 15 Andrey Yurlov/Shutterstock.com; p. 16 (chicken) Valentina_S/Shutterstock.com; p. 16 (chicks) Gelpi JM Shutterstock.com; p. 17 yevgeniy11/Shutterstock.com; p. 18 (couple) Andresr/Shutterstock.com; p. 18 (right man) Aaron Amat/Shutterstock.com; p. 19 Nanette Grebe/Shutterstock.com; p. 20 (left) Prezoom.nl/Shutterstock.com; p. 20 (right) Pete Pahham/Shutterstock.com; p. 21 Anton Havelaar/Shutterstock.com; p. 23 Panoramic Images/Getty Images.

Printed in the United States of America

CPSIA compliance information: Batch #CS15GS: For further information contact Gareth Stevens, New York, New York at 1-800-542-2595.